GW00367822

To:

Mum and Dad

From: Debbie

Just to let you
know how much
I love you xxxx

ISBN: 0-88396-969-6

Certain trademarks are used under license.

Manufactured in China.
First Printing: 2005

✺ This book is printed on recycled paper.

Blue Mountain Arts, Inc.
P.O. Box 4549, Boulder, Colorado 80306

I Miss You
So Much

Blue Mountain Arts®
Boulder, Colorado

Because We Can't Always Be Together...

I was thinking you might
forget how much
I care about you.
I don't want that to happen,
so I decided to send you
this little reminder...

*I love just being in
the same room as you.
I enjoy hearing your voice
and the sound
of your laughter.*

*Your happiness means
a lot to me,
and I am always hoping
that love, kindness,
health, and joy
will come your way...*

*Nothing can ever change
the way I feel about you —
not time or distance,
not anything you do
or don't do,
not anything I hear or see.*

So if you're ever lonely,
keep this handy,
read it again, and know
there's someone who always
cares about you... me.

— Barbara Cage

*It's Hard to
Be Apart
from You*

Each night when the world
is quiet and still,
   your smile
and the wonderful moments
   we have shared
crowd my mind.
Then I find myself
missing you even more...

Each day, as I go about
    my routine,
you slip gently into
my thoughts
and make me smile.
I wonder what you are doing
and trust everything
is going well.

*Though we can't be together
    right now,
we are together in our
thoughts and memories.
With all my heart, I am
looking ahead to that time
when I can see you
and be with you again.*

— B. L. McDaniel

If you are far away
and you need me,
then think about
the place you
love the most;
and if you are
tired or stressed or scared,

then meet me there...
in your heart,
and I'll meet you there,
in my heart...
and if that doesn't work...
just pick up the
phone... and
call me.

— Ashley Rice

When you care about someone
as much as I do about you,
being apart
is a hard thing
to get used to.

I thought I'd handle it
just fine...
and that I'd be happy
just to keep you on my mind.
But it isn't always that easy...

Sometimes the one thing that would please me the most... is simply seeing you.

I knew that I'd miss you.

*I just didn't know
I'd miss you
as much as I do.*

— Alin Austin

Though I don't write
or call you
as often as I would like to
I spend time every day
thinking about you
Sometimes it is
a memory of something
we shared

Other times it is
an incident in my life
that I imagine myself
telling you about
No matter what it is
in my mind
I write and call you
every day
and I miss you

— Susan Polis Schutz

Let's Keep
in Touch

Keeping in touch is a way
to say how much I would
love to brighten your day.
It is sharing a smile.
It helps shorten the space
between us
and reduce the time apart...

Keeping in touch is
a reflection of precious
feelings in the heart.
It ties together
the times of our lives,
the memories we have made,
and the dreams we're still
working on.

Keeping in touch is a way of making our strong attachment last a lifetime. It is a reminder someone cares and always will. Very much. About you.

— *Chris Gallatin*

Today I was reminded
of you...
taken back to a special
place in time...
And as I thought of you,
a certain sort of sadness
filled my heart...

*Even though the memories
we have are beautiful,
and thinking back on them
fills my heart with joy,
my eyes also swell with tears
because we are so far apart,
and I miss you very much.*

— Debbie Avery Pirus

You're Always
in My Heart

As each day breaks over my part of the world, you can be sure my thoughts will not be here — they will be with you, because...

The first thing in the morning, you'll be on my mind. As the day goes on... your smile will be present, I'll hear your laughter, and I'll think of you each moment, just as if you were right here with me.

And when the day is over, even sleep won't claim the loving thoughts within my heart, for in my sweetest and most precious dreams, you can be sure... I'll be seeing you.

— Barbara J. Hall

May the world
  hug you today
With its warmth and love
And whisper a joyful tune
In your heart

May the wind
  carry a voice
That tells you
  there is someone
Sitting in another corner
  of the world
Right now
Wishing you well.

— *Donna Abate*

I'd like to pack up
the greatest hug
I can give
and fill it with
as much love
and warmth as I hold
in my heart

*I'd send it across
the miles to you —
(stamped "Handle with Care")
in hopes that its magic
would surround you
and bring you as much joy
as you have given me
by being a part of my life*

— Elle Mastro

While we're apart,
I want you to keep me
in your heart
   and in your mind.

Just quietly close your eyes
once in a while
and imagine me here,
smiling and thinking
such thankful thoughts
of you...

For I spend so many quiet
moments of my own
thinking how much
I miss you,
  and how hard it is
    to be apart,

and how wonderful it is
that you're always
   with me,
warm and cherished...
   here in my heart.

— A. Rogers

*I Miss
Spending Time
with You*

❋

Every time we talk
on the phone,
I think of how nice it is
to hear your voice.
I love having the chance
to laugh together
and catch up on
    everything
that's been going on...

Whether we talk for hours
or just a few minutes,
our conversations always
   remind me
how much you mean to me
and how glad I am to have
someone like you in my life.

*But sometimes — after I
hang up the phone
and go back to my
daily routine —
I realize how much I miss
being with you, sharing all
the ordinary, everyday
experiences of our lives...*

I miss having you here
to cheer me up,
laugh with me
over a good joke,
or just sit and talk
about all those little
details we forget
to mention on the phone.

The bottom line is,
I miss you...
and I can't wait until
we get a chance
to spend some time
together again soon.

— Rachyl Taylor

Your memory
never leaves me.
There is not a day;
I could almost say
that there is not an
hour, when I do not
think of you.

— Gustave Flaubert

*Distance can never
weaken our
relationship...
For what is in our
minds and hearts
is stronger
than any outside force.*

— Susan Polis Schutz

You'll Always
Have Me
to Care
About You

No one ever really knows
what life has in store,
what roads lie ahead,
or how things will
    turn out...

It's kind of scary sometimes,
looking ahead and
   not knowing,
but I want you to know
that no matter where I am
or what I'm doing,
I will always have time
   for you.

You are very special to me;
you have a place in my heart
that will always be there
   for you.
You will never really
   be alone;
you'll always have me
to care about you.

— *Beth Fagan Quinn*

You're
Always
in My Heart

Take a minute
to think of me,
and let a smile
come your way...

*This smile has traveled
such a long way
and has
finally arrived
right where
I want it to be...*

There with you,
accompanied by
such nice thoughts...
that wanted to come along
on the journey.

— J. M. Colter

We wish to thank Susan Polis Schutz for permission to reprint the following poems that appear in this publication: "Distance can never..." and "Though I don't write...."